SHELTER

Homelessness
in Our Community

*Question, connect and take action to become better citizens
with a brighter future. Now that's smart thinking!*

SHELTER

Homelessness in Our Community

Lois Peterson

illustrated by Taryn Gee

ORCA BOOK PUBLISHERS

Published in Canada and the United States in 2021 by Orca Book Publishers.
orcabook.com

Library and Archives Canada Cataloguing in Publication
Title: Shelter : homelessness in our community / Lois Peterson; illustrated by Taryn Gee.
Other titles: Homelessness in our community
Names: Peterson, Lois, 1952– author. | Gee, Taryn, illustrator.
Description: Series statement: Orca think | Includes bibliographical references and index.
Identifiers: Canadiana (print) 20210095806 | Canadiana (ebook) 20210095938 |
ISBN 9781459825536 (hardcover) | ISBN 9781459825543 (PDF) | ISBN 9781459825550 (EPUB)
Subjects: LCSH: Homelessness—Juvenile literature.
Classification: LCC HV4493 .P48 2021 | DDC j362.5/92—dc23

Library of Congress Control Number: 2020951467

Summary: Part of the Orca Think series for middle-grade readers, this book answers the questions young people have about homelessness and its causes, effects, possible solutions, and what we can all do help.

Orca Book Publishers is committed to reducing the consumption of nonrenewable resources in the making of our books. We make every effort to use materials that support a sustainable future.

Orca Book Publishers gratefully acknowledges the support for its publishing programs provided by the following agencies: the Government of Canada, the Canada Council for the Arts and the Province of British Columbia through the BC Arts Council and the Book Publishing Tax Credit.

Cover and interior artwork by Taryn Gee
Edited by Kirstie Hudson
Design by Rachel Page
Author photo by LooRoo Photography

Printed and bound in South Korea.

24 23 22 21 • 1 2 3 4

This book is dedicated to everyone who longs for a better life—one of health, safety and security—and to those who work so hard to make it happen for themselves and others.

Twenty-five percent of author royalties from the sale of this book will be donated to the Nanaimo Unitarian Shelter in British Columbia, which has been providing men and women with a safe place to stay since 2008.

CONTENTS

Introduction

In the 40 years I worked in public libraries, I met many homeless people. I helped them use the library computers, fill in forms and find out where they could get a hot meal or medical help. On more than one rainy night I gave someone change so they could take a bus to a *shelter* that was holding a bed for them.

Later I worked as the executive director of a homeless shelter on Vancouver Island in British Columbia. I loved my job. I admired the hard-working staff. I appreciated the chance to meet our guests, who had such difficult lives through no fault of their own. I learned about other organizations providing important programs and services to people without homes, in my community and elsewhere.

I realized how much our society has to change if everyone is to be safe and healthy as they have the right to be. And I saw how many people have strong opinions about homelessness and possible solutions.

One of the thousands of homeless people who live on the streets of our cities and towns.
CINDY ORD/GETTY IMAGES

Encountering homeless people on the street provides an opportunity for kids and adults to talk about this social issue together.
FRANCO PAMPIRO

> "Each of us is just a human being like everyone else. We all desire happiness and do not want suffering."
>
> —The Dalai Lama, *Tibetan Buddhist head of state and spiritual leader*

The more we know, the better we can decide what needs to be done and what we can all do to help. It all starts with information and understanding.

How do *you* feel when you see someone you think might be homeless? Are you afraid? Or concerned? Are you curious about who they are and why they live that way?

I hope this book helps you learn more about the problem and encourages a kinder way to think about those who experience homelessness. I hope what you read here will help you be thoughtful rather than judgmental about everyone in your community, your neighborhood and your world. And that by the time you finish the book you will understand more about homelessness than when you started it.

Many homeless people spend much of their time going from place to place looking for somewhere safe to stay.
JUSTIN SULLIVAN/GETTY IMAGES

WHAT EVERYONE NEEDS TO BE HAPPY AND HEALTHY

Connection with other people is something we all need.
KATE_SEPT2004/GETTY IMAGES

In 1943 American psychologist Abraham Maslow released a study about what people need to be healthy, happy and safe. His theory is known as Maslow's hierarchy of needs. Maslow found that everyone has five basic needs:

Physiological. These are things our physical bodies need for survival, such as food, air, water and rest.

Safety. This includes feeling safe at home and when we're out and about, and being able to get the things like medical help and police services that keep us safe and well.

Love and belonging. Everyone needs friends, family and people they care about and who care about them.

Esteem. Everyone needs to feel good about themselves and be important to others. It's also important to be known for what we're good at.

Self-actualization. We all need goals and plans we feel we can achieve.

Most people have to get the first kind of needs met before they are able to get what's in the second type of needs. And only when they have the things in the second type are they likely to get those in the third kind. And so on.

THINK ABOUT THIS

What makes you feel happy?
Perhaps it's the people you know. A comfortable home life. What you do in the course of a day. Special times, things and events. Think about how important your family and friends are. Consider how food, water and rest keep you healthy. And how you learn and share skills and interests. How you celebrate special times and successes.

If you talk to your friends and family about what makes them feel safe, happy and taken care of, you'll probably discover that many things on their list are the same as yours. Now think about the things homeless people might not have. They might not have access to good food and safe water, medical attention or a safe place to rest when they need it. And consider the difference that makes to their lives.

SELF-
ACTUALIZATION

ESTEEM

LOVE & BELONGING

SAFETY NEEDS

PHYSIOLOGICAL NEEDS

One
Nowhere to Call Home

SPARE CHANGE?

On a cold, damp day, a man pushes an overflowing shopping cart along the street, talking to himself. Someone else sleeps under an old blanket in a doorway. On the ground is a piece of cardboard with the words *No home. No job. Please help.* On your way to the library, a woman reaches out to you. "Can you spare some change?" she asks.

These are familiar sights in many towns and cities. If you have seen homeless people in your community, you may have wondered, Why do people live like this? What do they need? What's being done for them? What can I do?

DEFINING HOMELESSNESS

A person is considered homeless if they don't have somewhere to live, or if they stay anywhere that is unsafe or not meant to be lived in. According to one estimate there are 150 million homeless people worldwide. In Canada, about 235,000 people experience homelessness every year, and in the United States, more than 500,000.

This woman is well known in New York's Central Park area, where local residents often provide her with food and clothing.
CHRIS HONDROS/GETTY IMAGES

Homelessness is increasing everywhere. A growing number of people are living in poverty, with no security, poor nutrition, not enough contact with friends and family, the risk of violence, and little access to healthcare, hygiene and **addiction** services.

Homelessness also affects communities. Family, friends and neighbors might want to help but don't know how. Businesses worry about losing customers if homeless people spend time nearby. Some residents don't feel safe with homeless people in their neighborhoods.

The United Nations Office of the High Commissioner for Human Rights states, "The human right to adequate housing is...the right of every woman, man, youth and child to gain and sustain a safe and secure home and community in which to live in peace and dignity." This is something everyone can agree on, and it's why so many people are working on the problem.

People living with an illness or a disability face challenges for getting around, which makes it hard to find a safe place to spend the day or stay overnight.
PEDRO RIBEIRO SIMÕES/
FLICKR.COM/CC BY 2.0

A SAFE PLACE TO STAY

Homeless people live in all kinds of places. In the bush. Under bridges. In deserted buildings. In cars. In alleys and parks. Some sleep in overnight shelters or emergency shelters. Others stay with friends and family for a while before moving on—this is sometimes called "couch surfing," which sounds like a lot more fun than it is.

There are the four levels of homelessness:
- Unsheltered—living in places not meant for human habitation, including abandoned buildings, doorways, parks and other public places
- Emergency sheltered—staying temporarily in overnight shelters
- Provisionally accommodated—staying in temporary places, such as with friends and family, but not staying long in each place
- At risk of homelessness—living in unsafe or unhealthy housing conditions, or not being able to pay housing costs

One estimate says that 36,000 homeless people live in downtown Los Angeles. Many gather in groups, taking shelter in tents and under tarps on any strip of land they can find.
SIMONE HOGAN/SHUTTERSTOCK.COM

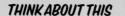

THINK ABOUT THIS

How would you feel if you had to sleep in a car?
What would there be room for? What would you have to leave behind? Where would be the best place to park the car? How would you get ready for school in the morning? If you told your friends, how might they react?

In 2017 a homeless count in San Francisco found that at least 1,200 people were living illegally in cars and vans. All over North America, people live in their vehicles, without access to washrooms or safe ways to prepare food, and most are afraid of being told to move on, as they have nowhere else to go.

HOMELESSNESS IS NOT A CHOICE

No one who is asked, "What do you want to be when you grow up?" is likely to answer, "I want to be homeless." Different life experiences and situations may lead to a person losing their home or not being able to find one. Anyone can find themselves homeless. But those who face *discrimination* because of their culture, age, health, abilities, language, religion, gender or sexual orientation may be faced with even greater challenges in finding a safe home.

But regardless of who they are, how they live and what caused their homelessness, everyone deserves compassion, kindness and consideration.

Adults

Most of the homeless people in North America are adults. Some gather in groups, while others keep to themselves, huddling in doorways for warmth and safety. They camp

Many people find a sense of safety and community through living near one another, but tent cities often attract opposition from other people living nearby.
DAVID MCNEW/NEWSMAKERS/
GETTY IMAGES

illegally in public parks, spend their time in libraries or move from place to place, carrying their belongings in bags and buggies. Those who live in the bush, under bridges or temporarily with friends or family are sometimes described as the "invisible homeless."

Challenges for Women

Willow's Place in Hamilton, Ontario, provides a warm welcome for women, whether they sleep on the street, spend the night in the nearby shelter or live alone. They come for a healthy meal and a shower, to do their laundry and to enjoy the companionship of other women, staff and volunteers.

Poverty is the main cause of homelessness for women in North America. For every dollar men earn at work, women earn as little as 79 cents for the same jobs. After they leave work, retired women who have no savings or don't get a *pension* may have very little money to live on.

Being homeless puts women at greater risk of violence, sexual assault and other crimes. Pregnant women who are homeless risk their own and their unborn babies' health if they don't get proper medical help or enough good food.

When families break up, women often take care of their children on their own. If they can't meet their children's needs or don't have safe housing, their children might be placed in *foster care*. This can create *trauma* that affects the mothers and their children for the rest of their lives, especially if they lose touch with one another or never live together again.

Living without a safe home can be particularly risky for women, who make up a quarter of the homeless population in North America.

Immigrants and Refugees

Sumiya Khan is the daughter of Indian immigrants. She knows how important meaningful work and relationships are to newcomers. Working with the New Haven, Connecticut, nonprofit organization City Seed, Sumiya formed Sanctuary Kitchen. The organization encourages women to gather to celebrate their own culture's food and provide a catering service and ready-to-go meals for the community.

Children are more likely to thrive when they have safe homes and adults to care for them.
SLADIC/GETTY IMAGES

Snapshot

Mickey

Mickey was 16 when his mom's *alcoholism* made home life so difficult that he went to stay with a friend. When he couldn't keep up at school, he quit and got a job on a construction site. But he was fired four months later after being wrongly accused of stealing. Then he was asked to leave his friend's home.

Mickey ended up living in a tent encampment with a group of people he had met in a park. He survived by moving from place to place, begging for money, doing odd jobs and eating at free-meal programs. After three years Mickey finally found a job and a secure place to live and began studying carpentry at night.

Newcomers to any country face many challenges when looking for housing and work.
SEAN GALLUP/GETTY IMAGES

It is hard for anyone coming to a strange country to have a better life if they face poverty, unemployment, poor housing and discrimination when they get there. Newcomers often settle in larger cities, where they have a better chance of finding work. But housing is usually expensive there, and families might have to share a small space. Housing can be cheaper in smaller communities, but there may be fewer jobs, which don't all pay well.

Indigenous People

For most people, home means a roof over their head. For Indigenous people, being connected to family, community, traditional land and culture is very important in creating a sense of home.

More Indigenous people are homeless in North America than non-Indigenous people. In Canada, 1.7 million of the country's 37.5 million people are Indigenous—1 of every 130 people.

In the United States, 6.6 million people of the 328 million are Indigenous—one of every 50 people.

But about 1 in 10 of all Indigenous people in both countries is homeless. And about one-third of homeless youth in North America are Indigenous.

A complicated history partly explains this. Indigenous Peoples have had their land stolen from them for generations. In the past many were forced to move to what are known as *reserves* in Canada and *reservations* in the United States. Children were forcibly taken from their families and placed in *residential schools* and foster homes. Children in these schools suffered abuse, were not allowed contact with their families and were forbidden to use their own language or practice their cultural traditions. Those experiences caused trauma and led to *intergenerational trauma* for their children, families and communities.

Loneliness and isolation contribute to the physical and mental health challenges faced by homeless people, who are often far from family and the community they knew.
BENJAMIN FONTAINE / EYEEM/GETTY IMAGES

Some Indigenous people leave their home community to find work or better housing. In cities and towns, however, they are often faced with landlords who won't rent to them, employers who won't hire them and health services that are hard to find. They might experience violence and have a harder time getting help because of the *racism* that exists in North America.

The work of organizations like Canada's National Association of Friendship Centres recognizes the history, culture and specific needs of Indigenous people. In Prince George, British Columbia, the Native Friendship Centre recently started a personal storage program, knowing that people new to the community often have nowhere to live and need a place to store their possessions and gather with people who share their culture.

Veterans and Military Personnel

To Tyler Stallings, the *veterans* in his family are heroes. When he learned that some veterans in his home state of Maryland were homeless, he wanted to build them houses. But he was only four! So he came up with a better idea. Since 2016 Tyler has filled "hero bags" with shoes, clothes, snacks and toiletries for people on the street and in homeless shelters. He has raised more than $50,000 and given out over 3,000 hero bags.

Men and women leaving the military often face challenges adapting to their new lives. They may not be able to find a job or a place to live. If they returned from wars and areas of conflict with physical injuries or mental health problems such as *PTSD*, it can be even harder to find work and a secure home.

A homeless US Navy veteran searches for clothing in his size at an event hosted by the Department of Veterans Affairs.
JOHN MOORE/GETTY IMAGES

Youth who are homeless are more likely to experience mental health problems and become dependent on drugs and alcohol than those who have stable, secure homes with family around them.
ZODEBALA/GETTY IMAGES

Youth

Because of invisible homelessness, there may be more than a million homeless youth aged 14 to 24 in the United States. In Canada, which has a smaller population, there may be as many as 40,000.

Some people think youth leave home because they want freedom and excitement. But most do it because they are uncared for, neglected, abused or experiencing conflict in their families. Between 25 and 40 percent of homeless youth in Canada identify as **LGBTQ2S**, and some of them are no longer welcome at home.

Whatever their reasons for leaving home, too often young people end up living on the street. A few might find temporary homes with foster families. But when youth in foster care "age out" at 18 or 19, they no longer receive housing, food and care. Without the support of foster families and the social services system, or if they can't find work or don't know how to manage money, many youth become homeless.

There are no statistics on the number of homeless youth who have to break the law to survive, as very few street crimes are reported. But about three of every four homeless youth are victims of theft, violence or abuse at one time or another, compared to about one in five people in the general population. So it is not surprising that some homeless youth develop mental health problems or use drugs or alcohol as a way to cope.

Most youth homeless programs are for 18- to 24-year-olds. There's less help for younger teens. Some homeless youth hide the fact that they are homeless, which might help keep them safe. But it also means they might not get the help they need. And, like most people without homes, youth usually face long waits for housing and services.

In 2019 two kindergartners in Ferndale, California, learned that some students at the nearby College of the Redwoods could pay their fees but didn't have enough money for housing. So on National Lemonade Day, Lincoln and Everly donated half of their lemonade-stand money to students who were sleeping in shelters, in their cars or on friends' couches. Planning ahead, Lincoln and Everly made sure to save the other half for their own college funds.

These two enterprising kids found a cool and delicious way to help local college students who could not afford a safe place to stay.
SONIA WARAICH—THE TIMES-STANDARD

HELPING OUT

Raising Money for a Good Cause
When he was five years old, Alexander from Calgary sold praying mantises to make enough money to buy a LEGO set. When his parents suggested that he donate half the money to *charity*, he chose Inn from the Cold. "I want to help the poor people," said Alexander. "Some of them may be alone or lonely or hungry." This organization continues to help families stay in the homes they have or find safe temporary and even permanent housing.

In Chicago, students from Queen of Martyrs Elementary School made Easter baskets for children staying at the local family shelter. Residents at the nearby retirement home filled the baskets with toiletries, candy and toys. The project was co-sponsored by the ward alderman's office. How's that for everyone working together to make a difference!

Children and Families

You won't see homeless children huddled in doorways in Canada and the United States, as you might in several other countries. But children make up about 1 in 5 of the approximately 50,000 "invisible" homeless people in North America.

Families with nowhere to live sometimes stay temporarily with relatives or in a shelter. Children might be left with other family members until their parents find housing. Some live with foster families until they can return to their parents. Living in difficult situations can be hard for kids for a number of reasons:

Without a good night's sleep, it can be hard to keep up with schoolwork.

Without enough nutritious food, they might get sick, miss school and fall behind.

Some kids won't make friends if they don't expect to stay in a school or neighborhood for long.

If their difficult life makes it hard to get along with other kids, they often feel lonely.

Doing well in school can be a challenge for kids who have to keep moving or changing schools.
SEAN GALLUP/GETTY IMAGES

Children without safe homes aren't the only ones with these problems. But children who are homeless are especially vulnerable.

If you are concerned about yourself, your own family or someone else you know, talk to a parent, teacher or trusted adult. If you don't know who to talk to:

In Canada you can contact the Kids Help Phone through its website KidsHelpPhone.ca, by phone at 1-800-668-6868 or text CONNECT to 686868. In the United States call 800-448-3000, any day, anytime.

The Elderly

About one in three homeless people in North America is 50 or older. Shelters report more and more senior guests looking for a place to stay. When the Salvation Army opened a 45-bed shelter in Etobicoke, Ontario, it was one of the few in North America specifically for seniors.

Happipad is a Canadian program that connects seniors who are having trouble paying their housing costs with

Making a call when you need help is the best thing you can do for yourself.
MRS/GETTY IMAGES

younger people who can't afford a place of their own. Sharing a home gives them both a better chance of being able to afford housing than if they lived on their own.

Isha Desselle, a senior in Houston used the money from the sale of her house to buy an apartment building. She lived in one suite and rented the others to seniors who needed an affordable place to live.

But not everyone is so fortunate. Once they retire from their work, many older people don't have much money to live on. Higher medical costs may leave them with less money for essentials, such as food and housing. Some states and provinces help older people pay their rent. But not all. And although some seniors qualify for affordable housing, there is not enough of it for everyone who needs it, and there are often long waiting lists.

As you can see, homelessness can affect anyone. The challenges each person faces are different. And the way out of homelessness is different for everyone too.

> "Never doubt that a small group of thoughtful, committed citizens can change the world; indeed, it's the only thing that ever has."
>
> —Margaret Mead,
> *an anthropologist who studied past and present culture and human behaviors*

North Americans view aging differently than people in many other countries that take greater care to ensure their elders are safe, healthy and well housed.
DIMABERKUT/GETTY IMAGES

San Francisco's Golden Gate Bridge is the famous landmark of a city that has some of the highest-priced housing in the country and more than 8,000 people experiencing homelessness.
JUSTIN SULLIVAN/GETTY IMAGES

Two
Everyone Counts

Communities all over North America run Point-in-Time Counts every couple of years to measure homelessness. People experiencing homelessness come to special events where they can get services such as haircuts, meals and changes of clothes. While they are there, they are asked how long they have been homeless, whether they have been homeless before and how often. They share information about their health, addictions, and how they earn money and spend their time. Workers and volunteers also go into the community to interview other homeless people wherever they find them. Information collected in studies like these is used by cities, states, provinces and federal governments to plan housing and services.

It's a challenge to get the exact number of people who live with poverty and homelessness. But we know that the number is too high everywhere. For example, on just one night in 2017 there were more than half a million people without homes in the United States. In Canada, an estimated 35,000 people were homeless on one night alone.

Volunteers working on Point-in-Time Counts go to places where homeless people live or spend time—such as under this bridge in San Francisco—to learn more about their stories, experiences and needs. JAN TONG / EYEEM/GETTY IMAGES

Jennie

Jennie is always cold. She's 69 and wears three pairs of gloves and a tuque, even indoors. "Can you imagine! People used to say I looked like a model!" she says.

Jennie has stayed in an Alberta women's shelter since her husband died. With only a small pension, she could no longer afford the rent on her apartment. "I've got a nice room of my own. But it's not home, is it?" She tried staying with her daughter's family. But the household is too noisy for Jennie, who has problems with anxiety.

She tells me, "I am on the waiting list for seniors' housing. I checked it out, and it's quite nice." Meanwhile, Jennie found out about programs in her community and joined the library book club. But she has not been in touch with her old friends lately. She says she'll be glad to invite them over when she has a new home and when she can wear some of her favorite clothes again. They aren't practical for her life right now, and Jennie keeps them in storage.

SO MANY STORIES

At five o'clock every evening, people line up outside the homeless shelter where I used to work. They come looking for a warm, safe place to sleep, a good meal and some companionship. Most nights, the 30 beds are full.

I got to know a few of the regular guests. Some had lived in the area for years and stayed at the shelter regularly. Others slept in different places—in a tent in the park, on a friend's couch—and came to the shelter when they had nowhere else to stay. Some guests shared their stories. Others kept to themselves. Homeless people often feel shame about the way they have to live.

Some people are homeless for a short time, just until their lives improve. Others are without a home for years. The longer a person has no home, the harder it can be to get one. This is why it's so important to prevent people from becoming homeless in the first place.

People find themselves without a safe place to live for a variety of reasons:

- The rent on their home has become too expensive for them.
- When they look for a new place to live, there are none they can afford.
- The only home they can find is unsafe or unhealthy.
- They lost the job that helped them pay their bills.
- Poor health prevents them from working, paying for housing or taking care of their home.
- They face discrimination from relatives or landlords.
- After a family breakup, they can't pay for their housing on their own.
- They recently moved for work and can't find a place to stay.
- After a lifetime of work and a regular income, their pension is not enough to pay for housing.
- Mental health problems or addictions prevent them from taking care of themselves or their home.
- After living on the street for a long time, they can no longer take care of themselves or a home.

Only by talking to this person can we know for sure why they are sleeping in the doorway and what they need to live a healthier, safer life.
JACK TAYLOR/GETTY IMAGES

Poverty

In the United States, a family of two making less than $12,700 a year ($35 a day) is considered poor. In Canada, a single person is considered poor if they make less than $18,000 to $20,000 a year—depending on which province they live in.

Without enough money, the necessities of life are hard to get. Poverty puts people's health at risk. They might not be able to take care of themselves or their children. Poverty affects their mental health and often damages their relationships with others.

Poverty is just one thing that affects people's lives. Other conditions can cause homelessness or make life difficult once people are without a home.

Standing in line for basic necessities is a common experience for poor and homeless people who have to rely on services like this church food program.
SPENCER PLATT/GETTY IMAGES

Drug and Alcohol Dependency

Once people start using drugs or alcohol, it can be hard to stop. Being unable to stop is called dependency or addiction, and it's actually a disease that affects how the brain and body work. Lots of adults in North America drink alcohol sometimes, but if they can't function without it, they could be suffering from alcoholism.

Addictions make it hard to find and keep a job or a home and get along with other people. In both the United States and Canada, about one-third of homeless people struggle with addictions. It takes a lot of hard work to recover, and it doesn't happen all at once. When they manage to stop using drugs or alcohol, most people see their lives improve. But it's hard to recover without help, and waiting lists for treatment are long.

Nearly 100,000 Americans die of illnesses related to alcohol use every year. People with substance-use issues who are also homeless have the most difficulty getting treatment.
CROTOGRAPHY/GETTY IMAGES

Mental Illness

Until about 50 years ago, people with mental illnesses were treated in special hospitals and live-in facilities. But hundreds of these places were closed when it was thought that it would be better—and cheaper—to treat people closer to their own families and communities. And at the time, it was also thought that new drug treatments for mental illness could replace the psychiatric treatment they had received in hospital.

But it turned out there weren't suitable places for everyone to live, or enough people or services to care for them. As a result many mentally ill people ended up without homes or support.

Mental illness encompasses a number of conditions that affect the way people feel, think and behave. Some of the most common are depression, anxiety and addictions. People affected by mental health illnesses can often be helped with medication and therapy—if they can find a doctor or counselor. But they might have trouble remembering to keep appointments or take medication. When people with severe conditions such as schizophrenia behave in ways that make it hard for others to help them, they have less chance of recovering.

The experience of being homeless may also *cause* mental illness in people who were healthy before.

MYTHBUSTER

"Homeless people are all drug addicts or alcoholics."

You might see homeless people swearing, talking to themselves or getting into confrontations with one another or passersby. Some of these behaviors might be caused by drug or alcohol addictions. But not everyone who is homeless suffers from these conditions. In fact, only about one in three people on the street are dependent on drugs or alcohol. Others suffer from mental illness, trauma or brain injury.

It's important to remember that even people with safe and secure homes, steady jobs and happy families struggle with addictions and other conditions we don't know about. Because homeless people are more visible, it can be too easy to make assumptions about them.

People who can't get the proper treatment for mental health issues, trauma or brain injuries may have greater problems finding and taking care of a home—and themselves.
MARTIN-DM/GETTY IMAGES

This football player runs a high risk of suffering a brain injury during the course of his career, which might lead to job loss and homelessness.
JPBCPA/GETTY IMAGES

Brains Can Be Injured Too

About half of the homeless people in North America may be affected by a traumatic brain injury. It may have happened earlier in their lives or since they have been homeless.

Our brain controls how our body works. If it is injured, our behavior, thoughts, speech and reactions change. This can affect relationships with friends and family. And it often stops people with brain injuries from working or taking care of themselves.

Traumatic brain injuries can be caused by accidents, violence or contact sports such as football or hockey. They sometimes result from severe illness, near-drowning or suffocation, or exposure to dangerous chemicals. Unlike broken legs, injured brains can't all be fixed. About 4 in 10 people with a brain injury may never recover completely, even with therapy and medicine. Staff and volunteers working with homeless people can't always recognize when someone has a brain injury, so people might not get the treatment they need.

THE EFFECTS OF TRAUMA

The word *trauma* describes a distressing physical or mental experience that changes how a person's brain works and how they cope with life. The trauma might have happened recently or a long time ago. It can be something a person talks about or something they have never told anyone.

Some causes of trauma are:

- Losing a parent or caregiver
- Experiencing physical and/or sexual abuse
- Being neglected, which means not getting the care a person needs
- Seeing something bad happen to someone else
- Being bullied or threatened
- Experiencing crime or violence
- Having a bad accident
- Serving in wars and other conflicts
- Living in a violent family
- Working as a police officer, firefighter, prison guard, paramedic or medical professional
- Being affected by the trauma experienced by earlier generations

HELPING OUT

Bringing Basic Necessities to People in Need

Bless It Bag, is an organization that helps homeless people in the United States. Its website offers handmade bags filled with essential items, which people can purchase to give to anyone in need. The bags include things like bottled water, underwear, food and even pet food. Plus, one dollar from the sale of each bag goes to a charity helping homeless people in other ways.

In Long Beach, CA, a group of women formed Beauty 2 The Streetz. In addition to providing showers and offering clothing and other essentials, they provide homeless women with haircuts and beauty-care products. As volunteers wash, cut and color their clients' hair, they help them feel valued and a little less alone.

Human touch and connection are important for everyone's health and well-being, and can make a big difference for someone who is dealing with mental health issues.
PEOPLEIMAGES/GETTY IMAGES

In the United States, about 200,000 men and women leave military service each year. Getting help adjusting to civilian life is very important if they are to find housing, work and medical services.
SDI PRODUCTIONS/GETTY IMAGES

A US study of homeless female veterans said that "homelessness and trauma go hand in hand." Whatever its cause, trauma can affect four out of five homeless people. It causes them to have difficulty managing their lives and sometimes leads to drug or alcohol use as they try to cope. With help, some people recover. Others are affected for the rest of their lives, which creates problems with maintaining friends and family, keeping a job and finding a permanent home.

TAKE CARE OF YOURSELF

People affected by mental health issues, trauma, alcohol or drug addictions or brain injuries might behave in ways that upset you. You might see them talking to themselves, moving in strange ways, or spreading their belongings all over the sidewalk. If you are concerned about a person you know or someone you have never seen before, remind yourself:

- You didn't cause their behavior.
- You can't cure it.
- You can't control it.
- You can care for yourself by sharing your feelings with a parent, teacher or someone else you trust, making healthy choices and celebrating your ability to take care of yourself.

(Source: Narcanon)

> "Never look down on anybody unless you're helping them up."
> —Reverend Jesse Jackson, *an American minister who works in the **civil rights** movement*

Talk to your parents and friends about how you feel when someone's behavior makes you uncomfortable. If it is caused by substance abuse, mental health problems or brain injury, remember that these are illnesses. They can't be fixed by telling someone to "smarten up" or "behave properly." But if there's enough help, everyone has a chance to be a little safer and healthier.

There are not enough mental health programs and services for everyone—which can either lead to homelessness or, once a person is homeless, make life even harder for them.
SEWCREAM/SHUTTERSTOCK.COM

Three
Life on the Streets

DAY AFTER DAY

One day when I was downtown, I passed an overflowing buggy with a shovel sticking out of it. A hand-lettered sign said, *I sweep and pick up litter. Please help with a cup of coffee or a meal. Thank you and God Bless.* The buggy's owner was sweeping leaves and garbage from the sidewalk.

Clent, who made sure I knew his name is spelled with an *e*, took on this job himself. "It helps out the neighborhood," he said. "And it keeps me busy." He has been homeless for years. "I camp in a couple of places in the bush," he told me. But he did not want to tell me exactly where, as he's afraid of being moved along.

Clent is just one of the men and women in my community who spend time on downtown benches or **panhandling** in doorways. They gather in parks and at outside café tables or move from one place to another, carrying all their belongings. Spending time together, they find companionship and share information—where to get a hot meal or a bed for the

This cart contains not only a homeless man's belongings, but also the rake and shovel he uses to help keep the street clean.
L. PETERSON

People sleeping in doorways are often forced to move along by business owners, customers or police officers enforcing loitering laws.
JACK TAYLOR/GETTY IMAGES

night, which areas are safe, how to get help for health and addiction problems.

Imagine spending all day outside, whatever the weather. Only a few restaurants, bus stations and other public places are open 24 hours a day. Libraries and community centers offer only daytime shelter. People often gather in parks during the day, but it's not unusual for local laws to prohibit camping overnight. Knowing how hard life is for homeless people on a day-to-day basis, you can probably imagine how much harder it was during the COVID-19 pandemic of 2020, when libraries, parks and public washrooms were closed.

When everything shuts down, or businesses won't let people stay for long during the day, the street is often the only place to go.

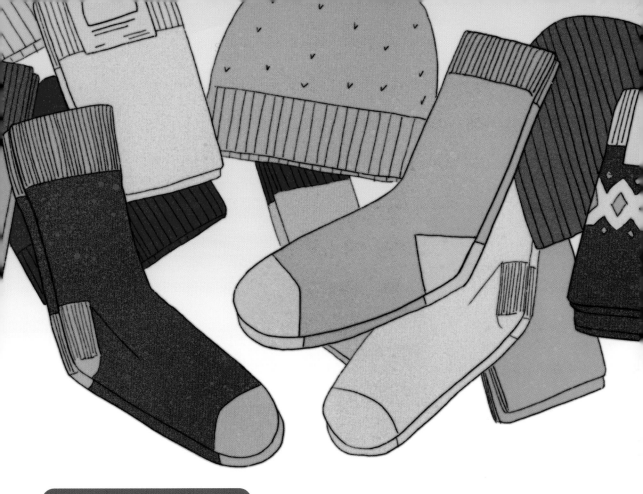

STAYING WARM AND DRY

Fifteen years ago, when Hannah Turner was just four, she volunteered at a community Thanksgiving dinner in Perrysburg, Ohio. She noticed a man wearing shoes but no socks. She was so worried about his cold feet that she wanted to give him her own socks.

So the next day Hannah and her mom bought 100 pairs of socks and delivered them to the local shelter. Since then Hannah's Socks has collected and given away over 10,000 pairs of socks and underwear to homeless people in the community. Hannah's generosity has inspired volunteers to help out too.

Nicole MacPherson of Nova Scotia came up with her own way of helping out. Instead of using ornaments, she decorates the Christmas tree in her yard with hats, gloves, sweaters and other warm clothing and invites anyone who needs anything to help themself.

Shelters and drop-in centers often provide coats, gloves and socks for their homeless clients, donated by local residents and businesses. Service clubs run clothing drives, where people donate clothes they no longer need. These might include warm coats, socks and hats, and even work clothes and boots for construction workers, graduation or prom outfits for students, or back-to-school clothes for children.

KEEPING CLEAN AND HEALTHY

Recently I noticed a homeless man going to the bathroom behind a tree. No one wants this happening in their neighborhood. But imagine the shame and embarrassment of not being able to find a washroom when you need one. Or having nowhere to clean your teeth or wash.

Poor hygiene affects people's appearance, their health and how they feel about themselves. That's why services such as the free shower program run by the City of Nanaimo, British Columbia, and Los Angeles's LavaMae[x] program, which provides mobile showers, hygiene kits and other essentials, are so important to anyone without a home of their own.

Almost half of all homeless people visit a hospital emergency room at least once a year,

Lava Mae^x provides free shower facilities and hand-washing stations on the streets of Los Angeles and also connects clients with other social services. The organization has helped set up similar programs in other communities.
JAVIER DE LEON

often because they didn't get medical attention before their illness or injury became worse. Some people won't visit a clinic if they weren't treated well on their last visit or if they expect to be judged for their lifestyle. People are sometimes discharged from hospital before they have fully recovered— even if they have nowhere else to go.

Homeless people don't always know when they need medical attention or where to get it. Mobile clinics treat people where they spend time, and medical staff detect and treat problems before their patients need more serious care. In Montreal, the international organization Doctors of the World Canada tests people on the streets for contagious diseases like **tuberculosis (TB)** and **hepatitis**. They give vaccinations and other treatment and make sure their patients know where to go if they need more help. The Jordan Valley Community Health Center in Springfield, Missouri, and the Vancouver Native Health Society in British Columbia treat homeless adults and children, sometimes even visiting schools and care homes. They provide care for patients where they find them and offer free or pay-what-you-can services.

Some people might prefer to spend their lives without a home if they don't feel safe in homeless shelters or if they need to be able to keep their pets or possessions with them. If they have spent a long time living outside, it can be hard to adapt to being inside.

A study in Toronto in 2013 found that 94 percent of homeless people in that city wanted a home of their own. And in the 2019 New Leaf research project in BC, 115 homeless people were given $7,500 each to find housing and take care of themselves. They were given training on how to budget and live a healthier life. After one year most had found safe permanent housing, were eating regularly, and were less dependent on drugs, cigarettes and alcohol, and some had even saved money for their future needs.

When we assume that people's situation is their choice rather than the result of circumstances, it stops us from trying to understand how they got there and how we can help.

From Maslow's hierarchy (see Introduction), you will have seen that a safe home is one of the most important things a person needs to be well and happy.

During the COVID-19 pandemic, a health worker talks with a homeless woman to ensure that she has the protective equipment she needs and knows where to get health and community services and supports. JOE RAEDLE/GETTY IMAGES

Canada has a universal healthcare program that provides free medical care for everyone, but it doesn't include dental care. In the United States, government programs such as Medicaid and Medicare pay the medical bills for people who are older or disabled and people who don't have much money. But patients might have to use only the specific doctors and clinics that governments and insurance companies are willing to pay for. And throughout North America, there just aren't enough doctors for everyone.

SLEEPING ROUGH

Sleeping rough means spending days and nights in such places as parks, doorways, alleys, under bridges or in parked cars—anywhere not designed for living or sleeping.

For a 2019 science-fair project, 15-year-old Montreal students Pasha Jones and Adrianna Vutrano invented a backpack that converts into a sleeping shelter. It's called a

Portable House. Pasha's uncle suffered from mental illness and was homeless when he died, so she knows how important it is to stay warm and dry. Each Portable House costs only $20 to make and keeps the sleeper warm in winter and cool in summer. Pasha and Adrianna are looking for a charity or business to mass-produce Portable Houses so that more homeless people can have one.

But many people, even those with blankets or sleeping bags, are often prevented from sleeping in public places. When I worked in a library, I woke a sleeping man. "Leave him alone. Let him sleep," another customer told me. She thought I was being unkind. I had to explain that staff wake people up to make sure they aren't sick.

We didn't have No Loitering signs in the library, but you may have seen them around your neighborhood. Communities often have laws or create obstacles that stop

Clinics like this one—which has been operating for more than 50 years—offer free healthcare and information to people without health insurance or the money to pay for treatment and care.

Snapshot

Cliff

Three years ago Cliff didn't have a home and was struggling with alcoholism. Now he has a place of his own in Nanaimo, BC. "It's been a bumpy ride. But I've been clean and sober for a year now," he says proudly. Like other people changing their lives, Cliff had to break with friends who shared some of his old habits.

Cliff is a member of the John Howard Society's Urban Clean Up Program. During his three shifts a week keeping the city streets clean, he also keeps an eye on what's going on around him. Recently he called an ambulance for a teenager who had overdosed on drugs. "No one else knew what was happening to him," he says. "I am glad I was there to help."

Cliff comes from a large First Nations family, all of whom live in the area. His nephew, who also was once homeless, now works with Cliff.

When anyone asks how he managed to quit drinking, Cliff tells them, "You have to use your own strength and willpower." His willpower and strength have changed his life. And everyone benefits from his efforts to keep the streets clean and safe.

Dogs are valuable companions. But people without homes or money often need help making sure their animals are well fed and cared for. GEOFF LINVILLE/STREET DAWG CREW OF UTAH

people from staying too long in one place. If homeless people sleep in public places—or just gather for company—they are often forced to move, threatened with jail, fined or taken to hospital against their will.

It's often safer to sleep in the open in the daytime. At night it's best for people to stay awake to protect themselves and their possessions. On very cold nights, anyone sleeping outside risks **hypothermia** or even death, which is why some cities operate special shelters during extreme weather. But there isn't always room for everyone, and guests will be back on the street again when the weather improves and the temporary shelter closes.

If you are worried that someone sleeping in a public place might be sick or injured, check with an adult who will know what do to.

FOR THE LOVE OF PETS

About one-quarter of people who are homeless in North America have pets. Animals provide love, companionship and protection for their owners, even though some people might wonder how someone without a home can take care of them.

When I see a dog sleeping beside a homeless person, I think about James Caughill. In 2016 he decided to walk across Canada with his dog, Muckwah, to let people know that shelters rarely allow pets.

People at the shelter where I worked know that pets are good for physical and mental health—especially for anyone suffering from loneliness or depression. The pets stay in a separate part of the building in case other guests have allergies or are afraid of dogs. But their owners can visit their pets any time, and the animals are as well fed and cared for as their owners are.

No homeless person should have to give up the chance for a safe place to stay because they have a pet.

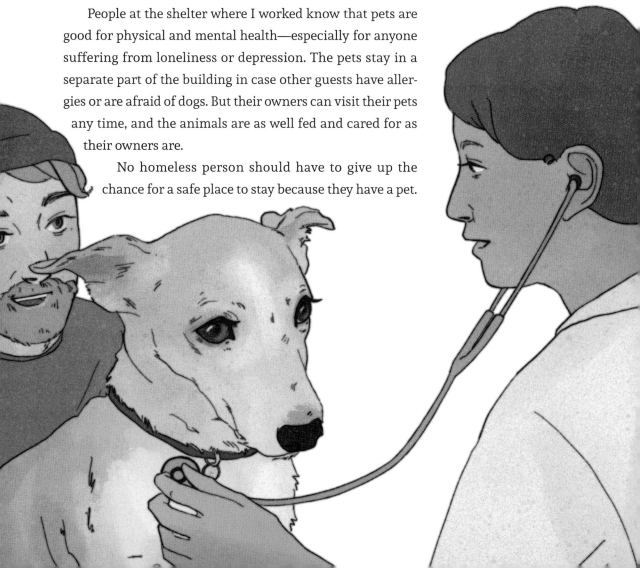

People use bags and carts to transport the things they need—items to help them sleep comfortably, a change of clothing and sometimes articles that could be sold to make money for important things like food.
JJFARQUITECTOS/GETTY IMAGES

PEOPLE'S POSSESSIONS ARE NOT GARBAGE

Do your parents ever ask you to get rid of toys, games and books that you no longer need? Deciding what to keep and what to give away can be hard. Imagine what it must be like for someone who doesn't have much to start with.

You may have wondered why homeless people loaded down by bags or pushing overflowing carts need so much "stuff." With nowhere to store it, most homeless people carry everything they own with them. Sleeping bags, blankets, garbage, food containers and drug supplies left on the street or in the park might be a sign that someone has been moved along by police or city officials without being able to take their possessions with them. Or it can mean there weren't enough garbage cans for them to clean up their trash.

THINK ABOUT THIS

How can you help the homeless pets in your neighborhood?
You could collect small stuffies to give away as pet toys or hand out dog treats. You could hold a neighborhood pet show to display your own pets and raise money to donate to organizations like the SPCA's Charlie's Pet Food Bank in BC or Street Dawg Crew of Utah. Street Dawg Crew provides veterinary care and food to dogs belonging to homeless people, as well as free vaccinations—so important in helping keep pets healthy.

Ask an adult to take you to meet pet-owning homeless people in your neighborhood. If you tell them about your own cat or dog, you will be sharing how pets help everyone feel safe and loved.

HANDLING NEEDLES

Finding discarded needles can be disturbing and dangerous. Here's what to do if you find needles in a public place:

- Don't panic. The fear of getting hurt from needles is worse than the actual risk—if they are handled correctly.

- Tell an adult, who will:
  - Put on latex gloves.
  - Pick up the needle with the pointed end facing away from themselves without putting the cap back on (if it is there).
  - Place the needle and the cap in a container with a lid.
  - Close the lid tightly.
  - Put the container in a garbage bin or needle-deposit bin, or take it to a pharmacy.

Most schools have guidelines for what to do about needles on school property or in the neighborhood. Ask your teacher what your school suggests.

No one likes to see drug paraphernalia in public places. But it is often a sign that there are not enough public washrooms or garbage containers in the neighborhood.
JEFF J. MITCHELL/GETTY IMAGES

SMALL CHANGE MAKES A BIG DIFFERENCE

I keep a stash of coins in my car to give to a friendly man with a long beard who often waits for cars to stop at the intersection near my house. Sometimes I have time to chat with him. On days he's not there, I wonder how he will eat that day.

People sometimes have to beg for money to pay for their most basic needs. This is also called panhandling. It may be the only way for someone to get money for food or a place to sleep, bus fare to get to a doctor's appointment or a shelter, or cigarettes, alcohol or even drugs.

Instead of giving money to homeless people directly, some people give to organizations that help them. They may think that if someone gets money by begging, they won't bother looking for work or will use the money for drugs and alcohol. I don't have other people telling me how to spend my money. Nor should anyone else just because they are homeless. I give money to panhandlers so they have the dignity of deciding for themselves what to use it for.

> "I raise up my voice—not so that I can shout, but so that those without a voice can be heard."
>
> —Malala Yousafzai, *a Pakistani teenager who was shot for speaking out in favor of girls and women receiving an education*

Giving cash or food to homeless people is a personal choice.
EVGAVRILOV/SHUTTERSTOCK.COM

This man seems settled on the street. But there is always the risk that he will be moved along at any minute by a business owner or police officer.
JEFF J. MITCHELL/GETTY IMAGES

Most people panhandling will be grateful for a sandwich or a cup of coffee. Some individuals and groups hand out care packages to people on the streets. These might include:

- A hat or pair of gloves or socks
- Food such as granola bars, pots of apple sauce or pudding
- A small package of tissues
- Toothbrush and toothpaste
- Body lotion
- Wet wipes or sanitizing wipes
- Bandages
- A comb and a small brush
- Nail clippers
- Lip balm
- A notebook and pen
- At Christmas or another special time of year, a coffee-shop gift card or a coupon for a slice of pizza
- At any time, a greeting card with a personal message

Panhandlers and homeless people often say that connecting with other people is just as important as receiving money. If someone says hello, asks how they are doing or takes the time to pet their dog, their day is a little brighter.

BOTTLE PICKING AND DUMPSTER DIVING

Every few weeks a young man rides his bike to the back of my apartment building to sort through the recycling and garbage bins. Somehow he manages to keep his balance as he rides away overloaded with bags of bottles and cans. It can't be fun rooting through trash. But bottle picking keeps recyclables out of the landfill. And the money that men and women earn by trading cans and bottles in pays for the things they need.

You may have seen people digging through dumpsters for things like clothes and food. One study found that grocery stores and restaurants throw away over 40 billion tons (36 billion tonnes) of food a year—almost one-third of the country's food supply! Organizations such as Food Rescue,

As much as 270,000 tons (245,000 tonnes) of garbage went into US landfills in 2018. Much of it could be used or recycled.
ANDREW BURTON/GETTY IMAGES

in Canada and the United States, help reduce food wastage and prevent hunger by finding ways to use the extra food from restaurants, grocery stores and food manufacturers.

Some places have trespassing laws against dumpster diving and bottle picking. Anyone caught doing it risks being fined up to $1,000, even though recycling is good for the environment, as it keeps garbage out of the landfill.

Four

Beyond the Basics

FOOD FOR EVERYONE

Having access to good food is important to everyone's well-being. But about 1 in 10 people in Canada and 1 in 8 in the United States doesn't get enough healthy food. Millions of North American homeless people—as well as people who have homes and jobs—rely on free breakfast and lunch programs, soup kitchens, food banks and *gleaning* programs.

Calgary's Sandwich Foundation receives food donations from individuals and businesses in the community. This food is distributed to schools and community groups, where students and volunteers make about 8,000 sandwiches a week. The sandwiches are delivered to shelters, drop-in centers and other places that offer people a healthy lunch. In San Francisco, Project Open Hand, the largest soup kitchen in the United States, provides more than 2,500 meals a day and hands out about 250 food parcels daily, relying on 125 volunteers to run the program.

In the United States, over 40 million people with low incomes qualify for the Supplemental Nutrition Allowance

Ten-year-old Cooper donates food to the food-bank box in his local grocery store. This is a great way for kids to help people who might not otherwise be able to afford healthy food.
L. PETERSON

53

Members of Universe City's food hub collect, sort and distribute donated produce to food banks and pantries in the Brooklyn borough of New York City.
SPENCER PLATT/GETTY IMAGES

> **"You can always, always give something, even if it is only kindness!"**
>
> —Anne Frank,
> *the teenage victim of the Holocaust who wrote* The Diary of Anne Frank

Program (called SNAP). They receive vouchers to exchange for food at grocery stores. But they have to have a job or be looking for work to qualify, so others still go hungry. For people with no way to make a living in Canada, income assistance (sometimes called **welfare** or **social assistance**) is meant to cover their expenses, but it's often not enough.

During the COVID-19 pandemic, a Vancouver Island school district provided food for 10,000 families a week—families whose kids would otherwise have missed out on school breakfast and lunch programs while school was suspended.

As a teen in Colorado, Chandra Starr put collection jars in schools and shops to raise money for Growing Food Forward, a group that plants gardens and delivers food to people who need it. Chandra beat her goal of $10,000 by $9,000!

Perhaps you have donated boxes of macaroni and cheese, canned fruit or cookies to a food-bank collection box at your local grocery store. Some places run Canstruction competitions in which teams create amazing sculptures with donated or purchased cans of food, and shoppers vote for their favorite. The food from these events is distributed to food banks.

The first food bank opened in Phoenix, Arizona, about 50 years ago. In the 1980s the food banks that opened across the United States and Canada to help people through bad economic times were meant to be temporary. But today food banks and smaller "pantries" still provide groceries to hundreds of thousands of people across North America every year.

THINK ABOUT THIS

What are libraries for?

In 2019 the Fredericton Public Library in New Brunswick installed a refrigerator stocked with fresh fruit and other snacks for people in need. Probably not what you'd expect to find in a library.

Libraries in such cities as Edmonton, Toronto and Seattle are helping their homeless customers by hiring social workers to help them find community services, including housing. Surrey Libraries in BC created leaflets with local information about housing, education, employment and income, food, transportation, health, household goods and legal services. Most libraries offer free use of computers so their customers can email friends and family, apply for services or look for work. Some let people without a library card or identification borrow books. Often a library is one of the few safe places where people without homes can spend time during the day.

Next time you borrow a book, check out all the things people are using your library for.

Hunger by the numbers

- There are over 700 food banks across Canada and 200 in the United States.
- The United States also has 60,000 smaller food pantries.
- In March 2019 more than one million Canadians used food banks.
- About one in three food-bank users were children.
- There were 46 million visits to food banks and pantries in the United States in 2019.

GETTING A GOOD NIGHT'S SLEEP

Emergency shelters are safe places for people without homes to sleep for one night or longer. Some are open all year, others only in cold or wet seasons. Some shelters are for men, while others are for women. Some shelters welcome both women and men.

Not everyone finds shelters comfortable or welcoming. Many shelters won't admit anyone who is drunk or on drugs. Not all shelters have room for guests' bikes or possessions, and not all accept pets. Shelters may be too noisy for anyone needing peace and quiet, and some guests worry about theft or violence.

Some people think shelters are too much like hospitals or prisons. But they do offer a way for homeless people to stay warm and dry, one night at a time, even though there are not enough beds for every homeless person who needs one.

Shelters by the numbers

- In 2018 there were 392 shelters in Canada.
- They provided more than 15,000 beds, with about 40 in each shelter.
- This was 9 shelters and 4,000 beds fewer than in 2016, even though more people experienced homelessness in 2018 than in 2016.
- In the United States in 2019, over 10,000 shelters provided about 555,000 beds, with an average of 50 beds per shelter.
- In Canada, 1 in 10 guests stays in a shelter for at least 30 days at a time.

People checked in to a temporary shelter in Las Vegas when the one they were staying in was closed after a guest tested positive for COVID-19.
ETHAN MILLER/GETTY IMAGES

ON THE MOVE

Kids should play in boxes, not live in them. That was the slogan for the 2019 Kids In A Box campaign at a community church in Manteca, California. Children decorated cardboard appliance boxes to draw attention to the need for safe housing for families and raise money for a local shelter. Youth groups, Scout troops and groups of friends stayed overnight in the boxes to help get the point across.

Women and children with nowhere to live or who are escaping danger often stay at transition houses or family shelters until they find somewhere new to live or it is safe to return home. There are similar facilities for single men and for people released from prison who have nowhere else to go.

As well as providing meals, showers and laundry services, staff and volunteers help guests find health and housing services, and make sure they feel safe. They might also offer help with child-minding, counseling or finding employment. But if there isn't a transition house in their own community, women and families have to move far from family and friends, which makes life even harder.

MAKESHIFT CAMPS

During the gold rush in the 1840s, men headed west to the Yukon and California, living in makeshift camps. In the 1930s, during the **Great Depression**, men and women crossed the country looking for work, building **shantytowns** on vacant land. These days millions of people escaping war, danger or famine stay in refugee camps until it is safe to move on.

Today in North America, homeless people create tent cities, areas with several people living in tents or under tarps on open land or in the bush. But tent cities are controversial. Neighbors often complain that tent cities are chaotic and dirty and encourage homeless people to move to the neighborhood. Others think that homeless people gathering in one place leads to crime and dangerous living conditions. They demand that tent cities be removed and everyone living in them moved along, even if there is nowhere else for them to go.

Cities and towns often restrict where homeless people can camp out, and some prohibit it completely. But encampments like this one on Los Angeles's Skid Row are common in areas where homelessness is high.
MARIO TAMA/GETTY IMAGES

Tent cities may not be the safest or healthiest way to live. But in some places—even in communities where residents don't want them—they are the most humane option for people who feel safer together rather than alone on the street.

A TALE OF TWO TENT CITIES

Anita Place

A tent city called Anita Place started in Maple Ridge, British Columbia, in 2017 to provide shelter for people without homes and to protest housing problems faced by people everywhere. Some neighbors were hostile. City officials took Anita Place organizers to court to try to close it down. The fire department confiscated owners' heaters and tarps.

Vancouver's Pivot Legal Society, which helps disadvantaged people by standing up for the human rights they're entitled to, represented Anita Place in court. The society even made a documentary about the residents' struggles, called *This Tent Is My Home—The Story of Anita Place.*

In 2019 the Government of British Columbia finally came up with a plan to build affordable housing for everyone living at Anita Place. Some people are concerned that there may not be enough homes, as more and more people are becoming homeless all the time. But new, affordable housing is what people living there have been fighting for and what everyone needs—a place to call home.

> "Just because a person does not have a home does not make them less of a person."
>
> —Resident of Anita Place, *Maple Ridge, BC*

Dignity Village

In 2000, homeless people in Portland, Oregon, started camping under a downtown bridge. The community, called Dignity Village, moved around the city for the next year. Later it split into three camps. One moved to an area called Sunderland Yard.

Snapshot

Jess

Jess stands outside the convenience store, holding a sign that reads, *Spare Change. Have a Nice Day.* On good days, he might collect $25. "That restaurant over there gives me cans and bottles to trade in sometimes," he tells me.

Jess has been on his own for eight years, since he was 15. He was in foster care for a while, but he left when he was not treated well.

He started taking drugs when he was 16 and is now trying to quit. "I got in with the wrong crowd," he says, so he's picky now about who he hangs out with. Sometimes Jess stays in a shelter, and he's found other safe places around town to spend nights. He likes to read, so he's a regular visitor to the library, where he can also get warm.

He has heard about some new housing going up in town. "One lady says she can get me on the waiting list," Jess says. He knows it will give him a better chance of getting help for his addiction and perhaps help to get training to work as a chef. "But it might be a while," he says sadly.

In 2004 a new law let municipalities set aside special areas for people without housing. Dignity Village was able to stay permanently at Sunderland Yard. The 60 residents take care of things like garbage and security. They organize food and clothing drives and make sure residents who need it get medical care. But there's no room for Dignity Village to grow, even though there are still people in Portland without homes.

ORGANIZATIONS AT WORK

Governments, ***nonprofit agencies*** and churches run so many programs that it can be hard to know where to go for help. But there are fewer services in small communities, so homeless people often gather in larger towns and cities, where they have the best chance of getting help.

Some cities publish directories of social services, either in print or online. In 2020 a new service called HelpSeeker started in British Columbia. The website and app provide information on thousands of social programs. HelpSeeker allows the people needing services and the staff working with clients to search by category—such as *food banks* and *shelters*—or by geographic area. HelpSeeker is most useful to people who have access to a computer or cell phone, which homeless people these days are likely to have.

CHURCHES SUPPORTING COMMUNITIES

You might not expect to see people sleeping in the pews of a church. But since 2004 as many as 200 homeless people each day find a warm welcome through the Gubbio Project, a hospitality and outreach program operated in collaboration with St. Boniface church in San Francisco. Worshippers use the front pews during church services. Anyone needing to sleep can use the pews farther back. They can also use the church washrooms, get warm blankets, socks, toiletries, showers and haircuts, and talk to a minister.

Knowing that people often can't collect welfare or pension checks or apply for work without an address, the Catholic Charities of Santa Clara County in California started The Window Program. It's a place in San Jose where homeless people can pick up their mail, use the phone to make appointments and find out where to get shelter, legal help and other services.

Churches, synagogues, mosques and other places of worship have a long history of helping people in need. They run lunch programs and clothing drives. They collect money from people attending services and donate it to organizations that help disadvantaged people. Some Sikh temples in

When COVID-19 hit, governments and organizations opened spaces like this one at Seattle Center's Exhibition Hall to provide shelter beds so people could maintain social distance from one another.
KAREN DUCEY/GETTY IMAGES

Canada and the United States offer free meals to people of any faith. Sometimes people of different faiths join forces to address social issues. In Toronto, for example, the Islamic Foundation of Toronto and the Darchei Noam synagogue run a breakfast program for youth.

WHAT GOVERNMENTS DO

Governments address the big issues that cause homelessness—poverty, the lack of affordable housing, and unemployment. They study the problems, make laws, plan programs and provide money.

When COVID-19 arrived in North America in 2020, there was concern about how it would affect homeless people. How could they socially distance? Where would they go if they got sick? What would happen if public places like libraries and community centers were closed?

In my city, this became a big issue for the local agencies that provide shelter, food, and health and outreach services.

No one had enough money to do everything that needed to be done. But gradually government funds started to come through to provide more shelters, temporary housing and food programs.

Services for homeless people are often partially funded by the government with money raised through taxes. But what is considered important by local and national governments—and residents—changes, especially in times of crisis. Some people want sports facilities or arts centers while others want better health services or improved schools, even though there's not enough money for everything.

Naturally, everyone working with disadvantaged people wants enough services to help them.

A number of voters, politicians and poverty activists are pushing governments to provide citizens with a universal basic income (UBI). This program would provide everyone with a specific sum of money, regardless of whether they work, what other money they have or what services they use. A UBI would ensure that everyone could pay for the basics in life—housing, food, health services and education. It would help prevent or reduce poverty and ensure greater *equality*.

When people can't count on a regular income to provide for their basic housing and health and nutritional needs, many rely on services like this food hub. SPENCER PLATT/GETTY IMAGES

Five
Not Wanted Here

I have often seen shoppers or businesspeople cross the street rather than walk past someone who may be homeless. Some of them object to people sleeping in doorways, sitting on park benches, visiting drop-in centers, gathering in tent cities, coming and going from overnight shelters or begging on the streets. Many people ignore those who are experiencing homelessness. Some threaten them. Others try to move them away. There are several reasons for this:

- They don't understand why others are homeless or what life is like for them.
- They are afraid of anyone who looks or behaves differently.
- Poverty and homelessness remind them of difficult times in their own lives.
- They might mistakenly believe that homeless and poor people are all criminals or drug users.
- They worry that people with mental health issues or addictions are a threat to their family and neighbors.

Store and restaurant owners and their staff rely on income from people paying for their services and goods. But customers often have to step over people living on the streets and in doorways to get to those businesses.
SPENCER PLATT/GETTY IMAGES

THINK ABOUT THIS

What do you see in *your* town or city that is designed to keep homeless people away?
If you look around your streets, parks and other public places, you may notice things designed to stop people staying in one place for long.

What does it say about how your community feels about people without homes? What do you think could be done to make sure everyone feels welcome? Talk to a parent or teacher to find out who you can write or talk to, to share your thoughts and ideas—a local politician or journalist perhaps. Sending a letter to the editor of your community newspaper is a good place to share your feelings about what's happening in your neighborhood and what you think should change.

STICKS AND STONES

I get upset when people refer to others who are poor, homeless or disadvantaged as "those people," "bums" or "deadbeats," forgetting that each person is an individual with their own story, problems and feelings. Everyone deserves respect, kindness and compassion.

You may have heard the chant *Sticks and stones may break my bones, but words will never hurt me.* And you know it's not true. Labeling any group of people dismisses and demeans them. The way we think and talk about other people *does* hurt. It hurts them. And it hurts us too.

"It was the community around me and the relationships and the love that people gave me that got me off the streets."

—Jesse Thistle,
author of From the Ashes: My Story of Being Métis, Homeless, and Finding My Way

"BUSED OUT"

Homeless people are often urged to "go back to wherever you came from." But many have lived in their community for a long time. If they did arrive recently, they probably came for the same reasons people have traveled to new places throughout history—to escape danger, flee famine or hunger, find a better home or job, or join family who have gone on ahead, seeking a better life.

One US study found that in an 18-month period, more than 30,000 people had either voluntarily or against their will been "bused out" of towns where they were staying, given train or bus tickets to other places. Sometimes this happens when big events like the Olympics or Expos are coming to a city. Officials worry that visitors won't come if homeless people live there.

Moving someone against their will is neither considerate nor compassionate—especially if they are forced back into danger or an unhealthy way of life.

ACTIONS SPEAK AS LOUDLY AS WORDS

Residents and business owners sometimes protest or sign petitions against social programs such as shelters or halfway houses. They believe that homelessness is "not their problem," or that other people and neighborhoods should take care of it. This is called NIMBY-ism. NIMBY stands for "not in my backyard."

Snapshot

Jennifer

Shortly after her mom died, Jennifer's dad told her to leave. So after she, her boyfriend, Nelson, and their dog traveled to Ontario for her mom's funeral, they moved to British Columbia.

Nelson found work, and they stayed in a homeless shelter while they looked for a pet-friendly place to live. When Jennifer got a job, they got their own place. But then Nelson got hurt and could no longer work. The income from Jennifer's low-paying job was not enough to pay their rent. When an affordable camper came up for sale on Vancouver Island, Jennifer and Nelson planned to buy it to live and travel in. But when they got there, the van had already been sold.

Now they are stuck living in their car. "We spend a lot of time in parks," says Jennifer. "There are bathrooms and parking lots with views. And we use the Wi-Fi at Timmies or McDonald's to apply for jobs." They either sleep in their car or at the local shelter.

"But it's really hard watching my life slowly fall apart and not seeing the light at the end of it yet," says Jennifer. She and Nelson recently headed to Manitoba, still hoping for work, a home and a happier life.

"A phone would be fantastic," says Jesse Vincent, a homeless man living in Nova Scotia. "In case I have to work or talk to my family or friends or, you know, if I ever have to call emergency services."

Cell phones are a necessity for nearly everyone these days. One estimate says three out of every four people who are homeless have cell phones. They use cheap pay-as-you-go services, topping up their phones when they have spare money. They log on to public Wi-Fi hot spots that give them free access to the internet. For Jesse, food and shelter are the most important things in his life right now. But getting a new phone comes close.

Soon after the COVID-19 pandemic arrived in Canada, the BC government gave away 3,500 cell phones so homeless people could stay in touch with family and friends while social distancing and managing their lives in difficult times.

If you look around your community, you might spot some of the things that are designed to keep homeless people away:

- Benches with arm rests so that no one can lie down on them
- Narrow, sloped seats at bus stops that are too uncomfortable to sit on for long
- Prickly bushes in planters to stop people from sitting on the planters
- Gated barriers to keep people away from buildings
- Locked garbage containers to prevent people from looking for food or recyclables
- Bike racks in alcoves and doorways to stop people from sleeping there

- Rocks and gravel sidewalks to discourage people from lying or sitting on the ground
- Raised grating on heat vents so people can't keep warm there
- Spikes on windowsills to prevent anyone from sitting there
- Loud music from hidden speakers to force people to move along
- No Trespassing or No Loitering signs on public property

When communities don't provide enough housing or shelter for homeless people, they resort to setting up camp wherever they can.
LEON NEAL/GETTY IMAGES

Lois Peterson

HELPING OUT

From Critic to Volunteer
In the 30 years Peggy Allen has lived in Abbotsford, BC, it has grown from a quiet farming community into a big, thriving city—with a lot homelessness.

Over the years Peggy has called the police more than 400 times to complain about people camping in the bush, drug activity or speeding traffic in her neighborhood.

She finally realized she was always angry. Wanting to change her attitude, she went from being critical of what was happening, to helping out. She joined a group called Drug War Survivors that works with homeless people.

Instead of complaining about social issues, Peggy started to share what she had learned with her community and soon became an **advocate** for the rights of homeless people. "Now I am solution-based as opposed to problem-based," she says. "Solution is good-feeling. Problem is bad-feeling."

The BC government established Newcastle Place, a supported-living complex, to house people who had been living in a downtown tent city.
ISLAND CRISIS CARE SOCIETY

GETTING TO KNOW THE NEIGHBORS

In 2018 the Ministry of Municipal Affairs and Housing in British Columbia set up temporary housing for people who had been living in a tent city near Nanaimo's waterfront. Eighty people moved into what look like renovated trailers at 250 Terminal Avenue. Some neighbors did not like this location being chosen or who would be living there.

But a group called Friends of 250 supported their new neighbors' right to be there. They learned everything they could about the housing and who the residents would be. At a rally, they provided facts rather than arguments. When the new residents moved into the complex, Friends of 250 presented them with welcome gifts of plants and household items and hosted community events to give everyone a chance to meet one another.

Their efforts did not change everyone's mind. But they encouraged people in the community to look at the situation in a different way and learn something about the realities of homeless people's lives. When an announcement was made in the summer of 2019 about permanent affordable housing being planned to replace the emergency units at 250 Terminal Avenue, everyone knew it would take a lot of work to make it succeed.

When local residents try to stop new housing, shelters or services for homeless people, they might be objecting because:

- They don't know enough about what is planned, how it will work and who it will help.
- They feel their own need for privacy and safety is threatened.
- They believe the people who might be helped by the service don't deserve it.
- They believe there are other important things that need doing.

It often takes community action like this to prevent foreclosures and evictions, which force people from their homes and can push many into homelessness.

Six
Paying the Bills

THE HIGH COST OF HOMELESSNESS

In June 2019 the Friends in Crisis shelter in Killeen, Texas, closed down when it did not have enough money to keep going. A young brother and sister made signs to let neighbors know what was happening. "We got lots of honks, lots of thumbs-ups, a lot of people rolling down their windows giving out donations," said their aunt, Linda Fletcher. The siblings have lived with their aunt since their mom died. "I told them she would be proud of them," Fletcher said.

Just four months later the shelter reopened, thanks to $100,000 in local donations.

Services to help people without homes cost a lot of money. Businesses often donate money and goods to nonprofit organizations and charities. Community foundations collect money, passing it on to the agencies running projects and programs. Service groups like the Lions and Rotary clubs and Soroptimist International raise money for programs and projects. People sometimes leave money to

Service clubs such as the Rotary and the Lions have a long history of raising money for services that help people live safer, better lives and improve the communities we live in.
JBK_PHOTOGRAPHY/GETTY IMAGES

Snapshot

Vince

The restaurants, public market and galleries on Granville Island in Vancouver, BC, attract a lot of visitors. When I'm in town, I like to drop by to see Vince. He lives in a rooming house and struggles with health and personal problems. But for the past 23 years he has spent several hours on most days in his usual spot outside the market. Here he talks to passersby and sells them the latest copy of *Megaphone,* the local street newspaper. Vince is especially proud of articles he has written himself.

The first **street newspapers** came out in the early 1980s. There are now at least 100 around the world and 10,000 vendors selling them. Street newspapers publish articles about homelessness and poverty, as well as politics and current affairs, often written by vendors like Vince.

Vendors buy copies of the newspapers from the publisher. Then they sell them for a profit of about $2 a copy. This adds up, especially for people like Vince, who has a number of regular customers.

their favorite charities in their wills. Fundraising campaigns raise money to pay for things like new buildings, food banks and medical equipment.

WORKING FOR A LIVING

One of the things contributing to poverty and homelessness is that not all working people make enough money to pay for their basic living expenses.

In Canada, each province sets the *minimum wage*—the lowest hourly rate anyone should be paid for any kind of work. It ranges from $11.32 an hour in Saskatchewan to more than $15 an hour in British Columbia. In the United States, the federal rate is $7.25 an hour, but in some places the minimum wage is higher—for example, $13.25 per hour in Washington, DC. Others, like Georgia, pay as little as $2.15 an hour for some kinds of work. Jobs that pay only the minimum wage—such as working in retail shops and fast-food restaurants—are often only part-time.

How's your math? If a person living in Edmonton, Alberta, earns the minimum wage of $15 an hour and works 20 hours a week, they make just $300 a week. Multiply this by four and you get $1,200 a month. They will actually bring home less than this, as employers take off money for such things as taxes and health or unemployment insurance.

Now deduct the person's rent at around $1,050 a month (homes cost much more in many places). That leaves only $150 a month for food, clothes, transportation to work or school, heat and electricity and phone. And it's certainly not enough for medical costs, entertainment and all the other things people need. This explains why for most couples and families—and even some individuals—one minimum wage job is not enough to cover all their costs.

"I hope you don't look down on people with disabilities, the unemployable, those who have no new clothes for job interviews, no updated résumés, the mentally ill, etc. Always remember: no one has it all together, but together we have it all."

—Vince Broad
in his November 2019 Megaphone *article*

Sears store employees lead a strike in Chicago, demanding better pay for people working in retail stores and fast-food restaurants, which often pay only minimum wage—not enough for a person to live on.
SCOTT OLSON/GETTY IMAGES

PUBLIC ASSISTANCE

Often the only money North Americans living in poverty get is from social programs administered by governments. Who gets it, and how much, depends on whether the person can work, whether they have health issues or disabilities, and whether they are supporting other family members.

Some payments are for a person's or family's basic needs, and some might cover rent but not much else. People receiving social assistance have to choose between buying food or paying rent, buying school supplies or new shoes. They may also worry about how to pay for doctor or dentist appointments.

Because most programs are run by individual states or provinces, how much a person gets depends on where they live. And the biggest problem is that social assistance does not keep up with the increasing cost of food, housing, clothing and everything else needed to live a safe and comfortable life.

Lineups like this at a New York food bank often include people who may have jobs or receive public assistance but do not make enough money for food.
SPENCER PLATT/GETTY IMAGES

LIVING ON A PENSION

A pension is a regular payment made to people on the basis of their age, years spent at work or a physical or mental disability. Nearly six million Canadians older than 65 receive Old Age Security pensions from the government. In the United States, 46 million seniors receive some kind of government pension based on their age or financial situation.

These are usually not enough to cover a person's living expenses.

Some seniors also get pensions earned through their years of work, contributing to either government or employer pension plans. People with physical and mental challenges might be eligible for disability pensions, depending on their individual situation and where they live.

But if they don't have savings or any other income, people may find that pensions are not enough to live on.

"Overcoming poverty is not a gesture of charity. It is the protection of a fundamental human right, the right to dignity and a decent life."

—Nelson Mandela, *former president of South Africa, who fought against* **apartheid**

On good days, a homeless person might make enough money to pay for a motel room for a night at a time.
HOWTOGOTO/GETTY IMAGES

Once they can no longer work, some seniors risk losing their homes if they cannot afford to pay their mortgage, rent or utilities bills as well as buy basics such as food, medicine, clothing and transportation.

RENT SUBSIDIES AND VOUCHERS

It is impossible to find and keep a home without enough money for rent and other housing costs like heat, electricity and hot water. A person or family whose income is very low might be eligible for a **subsidy** (in Canada) or a voucher (United States). This pays for some or all of the costs of renting a room, apartment or house, depending on the type of housing, the size of the family and whether adults are working or receiving other financial support.

But there aren't enough rent subsidies for everyone. And in order to get the money they need, people sometimes have to reveal information about their personal lives and their finances that most of us would choose to keep private.

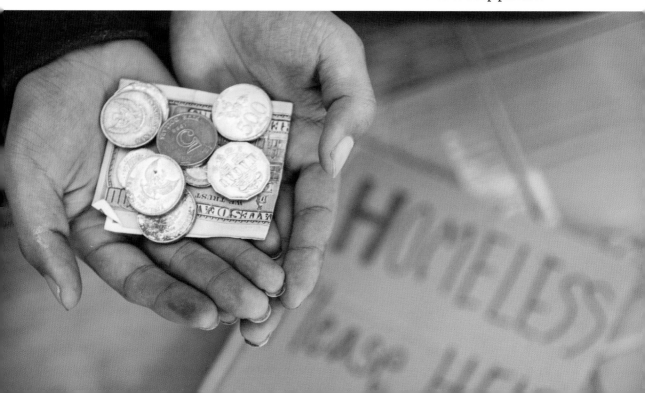

EARNING MONEY

Even without training or a regular paying job, many homeless people find ways to make some money, one way or another. It might not be enough to rent a home, but it can put a bit of cash in their pockets. For example, they might:

- Collect bottles and cans and trade them in to recycling centers and bottle depots for cash
- Sell things they find in garbage cans and dumpsters
- Take on odd jobs or small paid tasks for businesses
- Pick up one day's work at a time through a company that hires casual workers
- Help build a fence, sweep the sidewalk or move furniture for the shelter where they are staying
- Clean car windshields at intersections (this can be dangerous, and some cities have laws against it)
- Panhandle by asking passersby for change (which can be a humiliating thing to have to do, and many cities and towns have laws against this too)
- Sell street newspapers
- Buy and sell drugs

What was designed as a school playground is now being used by homeless people with nowhere else to pitch their tents.
TOM ALLEN / EYEEM/GETTY IMAGES

THE BOTTOM LINE

Providing the services and programs that help homeless people is more expensive than giving them a home of their own and helping them keep it. Police are often needed in communities where homeless people live on the street or in parks, even though much of the work that police do with homeless people could be done by workers who are better trained to help people with mental health, addiction and other social issues.

Hospital emergency departments provide expensive care to people who could have been treated sooner. Social service agencies are needed to provide counseling, employment programs and help finding housing. Addictions and mental health treatment can be expensive. Shelters cost money to run.

Ted Clugston, the mayor of Medicine Hat, Alberta—a city you will read about later—estimated that it might cost as much as $100,000 a year to provide homeless people with shelter and supports. But it would cost just $20,000 a year to provide them with secure housing—that's five times cheaper! Without a home, they are likely to need more health and addiction services, as well as a place to sleep and food. People with a home are likely to be healthier, find work, eat well, manage their addictions better and rely less on social programs.

Homelessness costs a lot, not just financially, but also in the cost to human life and dignity.

Ensuring that this man has a safe place to live might be cheaper than providing him with all the services and supports he needs if he is homeless.
DREW ANGERER/GETTY IMAGES

Finding a Job
Getting work is an important step toward being able to pay for a secure home. But homeless people often need to learn new skills, find jobs that suit them and learn how to apply for them.

A New York program supports recently released prisoners who don't have a home or suffer from substance abuse. Ready, Willing & Able teaches them how to do specific jobs in the service or construction industry and helps them find work. The 12-month program is residential, so clients have somewhere to stay while they go through the program.

WHAT WOULD YOU BUY?

One winter when I was running the shelter, I was asked, "What would you do with a donation of $10? What about a donation of $5,000?"

The first question was easy to answer. When guests arrive at the shelter, they are often cold and wet. "Socks. We'd buy a pair of socks," I said. "Or three pairs, if we could get a good deal." Foot health is important to the overall health of homeless people, and the shelter gives away dozens of pairs of socks each season.

What could we do with $5,000? The shelter's basic costs are covered by government funding. The building is in pretty good shape. The fridge, stove, dishwasher, washers and dryers work well. Donations help pay for special supplies and equipment. The shelter gets good deals on food, to provide two healthy meals to everyone each day.

The shelter has enough money to provide the basics—a warm bed, healthy meals, clean laundry and companionship for its guests. But they often need other supports. Some have untreated illnesses or addictions. Others are looking for work. Some need help with their mental health and trauma problems. Others just need somewhere to go in the daytime and caring compassionate people to talk to. And nearly every guest would like a home of their own.

Five thousand dollars would buy a lot of socks. But in the end, I said the best use of the money would be for the shelter's outreach program. It connects shelter guests with health and financial services to help them be safe and healthy and tries to find them permanent housing.

As many as 2,000 people wait in line to receive help each time this mosque and cultural center in New York City distributes free food.
SPENCER PLATT/GETTY IMAGES

Seven
Housing First

WHICH COMES FIRST, HOUSING OR HEALTH?

Some people believe that every person needs a home before they can improve their health, deal with addictions or find work. This is the Housing First model, used in many countries, states and provinces. Others people think homeless persons shouldn't have a home until they have solved their problems. Sadly, there are even some who think that homeless adults—especially anyone with drug and/or alcohol problems—should not be "rewarded" with housing, forgetting that safe housing is a basic human right.

KR lived under a bridge for five years before he found a place to live in 2017. He is now settled and safe enough to take care of his health problems. He is lucky to live in a city that is committed to solving the problem of poverty and homelessness. Since 2009 Medicine Hat, Alberta, has created new homes and provided shelters for 1,200 homeless people. Within three days of losing their home, each person is seen by a social worker, who helps them find housing within 10 days.

There are differing views on whether people should get help dealing with addictions and mental health challenges before they are provided with housing, but homeless people still need somewhere to sleep every night.
CARLOS ALVAREZ/GETTY IMAGES

"We don't see the homeless on the streets like they do in Calgary, Edmonton, Vancouver, the bigger centers," says Murray Kumm of the Hope Street Compassionate Ministry Centre. Even though the city has come as close as any in Canada to solving homelessness, there are still people in Medicine Hat who have to couch surf at friends' houses or live in cars.

HOUSING

As a huge apartment complex with 200 units was going up on my street, I wondered, Who will be able to afford to live there? Nanaimo, British Columbia, where I live, has many homeless people, and housing prices keep going up.

Market housing, about 95 percent of all housing in British Columbia, rents or sells at prices that only people with steady decent-paying jobs can afford. On the other hand, affordable housing is most often owned and run by governments or nonprofit agencies. At most, renters are charged one-third of their income. Historically this was thought to be the most that *anyone* should be paying for housing,

Not all single rooms in rooming houses are well maintained, hygienic and safe.
L. PETERSON

THINK ABOUT THIS

What can you do?
In Ottawa, Operation Come Home runs a program called BottleWorks. Staff and volunteers collect empty bottles and cans from restaurants, bars, hotels and conference centers. The money raised by trading them in helps fund Operation Come Home's youth homelessness and job-training programs.

If you look around your community, you'll see lots of things others are doing to help people in need. They include running bottle drives to raise money for playground equipment, school band trips, churches and homeless shelters. One recyclable bottle or can in your house might be worth only 10 cents, but the money soon adds up when everyone pitches in to raise funds for a good cause.

If you don't want to run a bottle drive yourself, round up all the recyclables you have at home, take them to the recycling center and make a donation to a cause that means something to you. What would that be?

Rental Housing Works

Affordable Housing and Jobs
for Maryland Families

A program of the
Maryland Department of
Housing and Community
Development

but even one-third is too much these days for people with low incomes. In Canada, less than one-fifth of houses and apartments are considered affordable housing.

As you have learned, one of the main reasons for homelessness is that there is not enough housing that everyone can afford. Until they find a safe place where they can manage their own lives, some people move from one type of housing to another.

Transition houses and halfway houses are usually for women and children who need a safe place to stay until their lives improve. Some are for men or women after they are released from prison.

Recovery houses are for adults who need help overcoming addictions.

Emergency shelters (see chapter 4) provide a bed for a night or longer for people who have nowhere else to go.

In supported housing, staff help each resident find the services they need to get healthy, deal with addiction,

Even with new developments like this, it is hard to keep up with the demand for safe housing in many communities.
MARYLAND GOVPICS/FLICKR.COM/CC BY 2.0

find work and take care of their own home. As residents' lives improve in this type of housing, they have a better chance of living successfully on their own.

Single-room occupancy hotels, rooming houses or hostels provide rented rooms for people who might live there permanently—often with shared kitchens and bathrooms. If the owners care more about making money than providing good housing, they may not take care of the property or treat tenants well.

MAKING IT WORK

Anyone who rebuilds their life after being homeless has a lot to be proud of. But it may have taken a long time to find the right home. If someone has not lived on their own for a while, they might find it difficult to manage their money and take care of a home. It can be hard to live alone without friends or family nearby. Having services and people to support them gives people the best chance to succeed.

A colleague at another agency told me that one client tried living in six different housing situations before they finally found an apartment that was affordable and secure enough for them to stay there. Some people have a home for a while, then something happens and they lose it, and they have to start all over again. But those who make the adjustment to taking care of themselves and their own home have a better chance for a happy and productive life.

WHOSE JOB IS IT?

Whenever someone says, "No one is doing anything about homelessness," I think about everyone who gathers at monthly meetings of the Nanaimo Homeless Coalition. Like similar groups all over North America, it represents a number of agencies working to improve life for people experiencing homelessness.

Many people are working to develop different types of affordable homes—such as these converted shipping containers.
CHRIS J RATCLIFFE/GETTY IMAGES

In 2016 the Canadian Observatory on Homelessness found that more than a quarter of a million people worked in homelessness, social services and community services. At least 10,000 of them work directly with homeless people. Some are social workers, counselors or specialists in addictions or mental health. Some are managers and fundraisers. Others are researchers who study the issue of homelessness and share information with governments and funders.

Some people have no formal training, but they use skills from other jobs to support people experiencing homelessness or living with addiction or mental health problems. Some helpers with *lived experience* have been homeless themselves or have experienced violence, addiction or mental health challenges. They understand what others are going through and use what they know to help them.

Doctors Without Borders/Médecins Sans Frontières runs this temporary shower program in New York. It's just one of hundreds of organizations whose staff and volunteers provide services to homeless people.
SPENCER PLATT/GETTY IMAGES

Snapshot

Don's Happy Ending

Don had been living in his car and using the free shower program at a city park, run by the shelter where I worked. One morning he dropped by to tell staff that he had finally found a place to live.

It had taken him a while. His pension was enough to pay for basic housing. But he had no references from other places he'd stayed—which landlords check to be sure tenants can pay their rent and take care of their home. He had lived in his car, even driving across Canada when he heard that housing was cheaper in Ontario. It wasn't, so he came back to BC.

In the past Don had been in single-room-occupancy housing, which he left because the building was falling apart. He did not stay in shelters, as there was nowhere to store his things. He had lived in a tent in the bush from time to time, but each time had been moved on by police.

With winter approaching, Don knew he could not live outdoors any longer.

When he was asked how he had found a place to live, his face creased in a slow smile. "It's thanks to the people working here," he said. The staff had suggested that instead of answering advertisements for apartments, Don could write his own, explaining who he was and what he needed.

It wasn't long before he was contacted by two women who needed someone to share their apartment to help pay the rent. They didn't need references or his private financial information. When they met him, they could tell he would be a quiet, responsible tenant.

Don thinks he will be able to settle down now for a while. Meanwhile, with three people sharing the rent, three fewer people are at risk of being homeless.

OUTREACH WORKERS

Forty-seven-year-old Jamie has been homeless for so long that he has lost most of the things he once owned. Sometimes when he moves he can't take the few things he still has with him, and a lot has been stolen from him. Recently he lost his wallet. His identification was inside, which Jamie needs for signing up for financial or medical help. Jamie needed help, and that's when ***outreach workers*** stepped in.

They go to the places in the community where home-less people gather rather than expecting homeless people to find them. They know about housing, health and employment services. They help clients fill out forms, get to appointments and get financial assistance that they are entitled to. They know about programs for treating addictions or mental health problems. Outreach workers sometimes help their clients find housing and set up and take care of their homes so they can keep them.

ADVOCATES

To advocate for someone is to act or speak on their behalf, to make sure their rights are respected and that they get the legal and social supports they are entitled to. Poverty and homelessness advocates help change laws and create policies about services and programs and work to make sure everyone gets them. Some advocates work for agencies such as the Anti-Poverty Committee in Vancouver, British Columbia, or Street Roots in Portland, Oregon, that address the underlying causes of poverty and homelessness.

Others work for organizations that provide specific programs such as health, housing or employment services.

Advocates understand the challenges faced by their clients. They explain homelessness to people who don't know much about it and get governments to provide help. They encourage everyone to look for a solution and to speak up for themselves if they can.

Writer Jesse Thistle is one of the most well-known homelessness advocates in Canada. He speaks at conferences and wrote a bestselling book called *From the Ashes: My Story of Being Métis, Homeless, and Finding My Way,* which gives readers an inside look at what it is like to live without a safe, secure home.

Jesse Thistle is an author and activist who has experienced homelessness himself.
LUCIE PEKAREK-THISTLE/WIKIMEDIA COMMONS/CC BY-SA 4.0

IN PRAISE OF VOLUNTEERS

At the Nanaimo Unitarian Shelter, everyone loved Val and Debbie's shepherd's pie, lasagna and macaroni and cheese. Every Thursday for over a year, these volunteers made and served dinner for 30 shelter guests. They enjoyed helping

Former first lady of the United States Michelle Obama works alongside other volunteers at Miriam's Kitchen in Washington, DC, serving meals to homeless members of the community.
WIN MCNAMEE/GETTY IMAGES

other people and sharing their cooking. Val and Debbie moved on to do other things, but every month other people in the community call the shelter, wanting to know how they can help.

About one in three Canadian adults volunteers. In the United States, it's about one in four. Volunteers help immigrants settle into new communities, teach children and adults to read, put on community events, coach sports or teach the arts. They clean up streets, parks and rivers, deliver books to people who can't get to the library or drive patients to medical appointments.

Soup kitchens and emergency shelters are often run by volunteers. There are volunteers who collect and deliver warm clothes to shelters. Some raise money for new buildings or programs or provide childcare while mothers look for work or get counseling. Professional health workers volunteer medical and dental care. And a lot of volunteers help run the homelessness Point-in-Time Counts, collecting information that is used to plan new services.

People from all over the world go to India to volunteer at Mother Teresa's Missionaries of Charity organization in Calcutta, India. Every night she searched the streets for homeless people who were ill and took them to her hospital, making sure they would not die alone. But not everyone wanting to volunteer has to go to India. There's lots to do closer to home.

In my first volunteer position as a crisis-line counselor, I talked to lots of callers. Some just wanted someone to talk to. Others needed to know how to find a place to stay, get medical help, or find a hot meal. Volunteering gave me a sense of how much help was out there in the community and taught me that everyone can contribute to making other people's lives better.

"I alone cannot change the world, but I can cast a stone across the waters to create many ripples."

—Mother Teresa,
who cared for ill and dying people in Calcutta, India

HOMELESS PEOPLE HELPING THEMSELVES

More than 1,500 people attended a Canadian Alliance to End Homelessness conference in Edmonton in 2019, including me. I met researchers, funders and staff and volunteers from all over Canada. At least 100 people who attended workshops and spoke on panels had once been homeless themselves or were still struggling to find a home.

In the past "experts" figured out what people needed, then worked to get it for them. These days people who are now or at one time have been homeless are involved in helping themselves and others like them, in different roles. They might:

- Run food banks, shelters or community agencies
- Share their stories so other people can better under-stand homelessness
- Volunteer at clothing drives, food banks and meal programs
- Write letters to newspapers and government officials
- Work in shelters, housing complexes, food banks and social service agencies
- Provide information to governments and people with power
- Become researchers, business leaders and politicians

Volunteers pack fresh produce from Corbin Hill Food Project to be distributed to food banks in the Brooklyn borough of New York City.
SPENCER PLATT/GETTY IMAGES

People working together can produce amazing results and help solve many of society's problems.
HILL STREET STUDIOS/GETTY IMAGES

A HAND UP OR A HANDOUT?

Imagine that your room is a mess. Your friend is coming to stay, and she needs to sleep in your bed. Your job is to clean it up before she comes. Your sister takes pity on you, making your bed, picking up your clothes and vacuuming the floor. Is your sister giving you a handout or a hand up?

Turning Plastic Bags into Sleeping Mats

How crafty are you? Amazing and useful things can be made out of stuff that otherwise would get thrown away. In Colorado a group called Bev's Bag Brigade has been crocheting sleeping mats for homeless people since 2009. The mats are made with "plarn," a plastic yarn created by cutting plastic bags into strips and tying them together into a long strand that can be crocheted or woven.

You can learn how to make them yourself by searching for plarn videos on YouTube. It takes a lot of plastic bags to make one mat, so you could involve your friends, classmates and family in collecting bags for making plarn. And then, together, you can come up with a way to give your finished mats to people who might need them.

A *handout* requires little of the person with the problem. But giving someone a *hand up* encourages them to do what they need to do, so they can do it themselves next time. Some people think that if people get something for free, or with little effort, they won't appreciate it as much as if they had worked or paid for it themselves. Anyone in need—of money, housing, food, clothing or work—benefits most if they have played some part in making their own life better.

As Maslow's hierarchy of needs shows, having confidence and self-respect is important to everyone.

It upsets me when people say, "The problem is so big, no one can make a difference." Throughout this book, you have seen how people are being helped by government programs, organizations, staff, volunteers, donors and caring adults and kids like you.

Governments and people with power and money still need to do more to address the problems that cause homelessness. Until then people will continue to struggle with all the issues that cause it in the first place.

But if everyone does something, however small, more people will get helped in more ways. And so will our neighborhoods and communities.

Start here: Share what you may have learned in this book with other kids and adults in your life. Instead of looking away when you pass a homeless person on the street, take a moment to smile. If you feel comfortable, say hello. Pet their dog. You might even ask how they are doing.

It could make all the difference to them. And to you. And to the world we all share.

GLOSSARY

addiction—an ongoing physical and mental dependence on a substance, such as drugs or alcohol, or a behavior, such as gambling

advocate—a person who speaks out on behalf of another person or group to solve a particular problem and change laws

alcoholism—a disorder in which someone drinks too much alcohol and is unable to stop

apartheid—a system originating in South Africa for keeping people from one race/ethnic group separated from people of another race/ethnic group and condoning the discrimination of one group against the other

charity—an organization whose goal is to provide services rather than make money; also called a nonprofit agency

civil rights—rights that citizens have under government laws not to be discriminated against, regardless of gender, skin color, religion, nationality, age, disability or sexual orientation

discrimination—the unfair treatment of one person or group of people; also called prejudice

equality—the state of everyone having the same rights, treatment and access to what they need

foster care—a system in which children and youth who can't live with their birth families are placed under the care of others, either in private homes or group homes

gleaning—the act of collecting and donating extra fruit, vegetables and other produce from farms, gardens and orchards to people who can't afford to buy fresh food

Great Depression—a time in history when bad weather, poor harvests and failing banks led to people losing their savings, jobs and homes

hepatitis—an infectious disease that affects the liver

hypothermia—a dangerous drop in body temperature, caused by being cold for too long

intergenerational trauma—the effects of untreated trauma experienced by earlier generations (parents, grandparents, etc.) that continue to affect younger generations in the family and the community. See *trauma*.

LGBTQ2S—lesbian, gay, bisexual, transsexual, queer, Two Spirit

lived experience—personal knowledge gained through direct, first-hand involvement in particular events or situations

minimum wage—government-set minimum hourly pay that people should receive for work

nonprofit agencies—organizations whose goal is to provide services rather than make money

outreach workers—trained staff who go out into the community to connect with people who need help rather than expecting them to come to where the services are

panhandling—begging for money or food

pension—money paid to people who have retired after working in a particular job for a long time or have quit working because of their age or physical condition

PTSD—abbreviation for post-traumatic stress disorder, a mental health condition caused by trauma

racism—the belief that people of certain races, cultures or ethnicities are inferior and therefore deserving of being treated with less kindness, respect and consideration

reservations—land Native Americans were forced to live on as the White settlers took control of their traditional territories

reserves—land First Nations were forced to live on as the White settlers took control of their traditional territories

residential schools—government-sponsored, church-run schools that Indigenous children were forced to attend, where they were separated from family and community, were prevented from using their own language, suffered physical as well as emotional abuse and in many cases died. These schools existed in Canada from the 1830s to the 1990s.

social assistance—a government program that provides regular financial support to people with no other way to make a living; sometimes called welfare or income assistance

shantytowns—settlements of shacks and other temporary housing with no proper services such as sanitation and water

shelter—a place that provides a bed for the night to someone without a home

street newspapers—publications created by and for people who live on the street, who sell them for a profit

subsidy—a grant of money, usually from the government, to help pay for things like housing or childcare; sometimes called a voucher

trauma—a distressing physical or mental experience that affects a person's mental and/or physical health and well-being

tuberculosis (TB)—an infectious disease that affects the lungs

veterans—men and women who served in the armed forces

welfare—a government program that provides financial support to people with no other way to make a living; sometimes called income assistance or social assistance

RESOURCES

Books—Nonfiction

Claybourne, Anna. *Healthy for Life: Smoking, Drugs and Alcohol.* London, UK: Hachette Children's Group, 2018.

Featherstone, Ann, Suzanne Del Rizzo, et al. *A World of Kindness.* Toronto, ON: Pajama Press, 2018.

Irvine, Leslie. *My Dog Always Eats First: Homeless People & Their Animals.* Boulder, CO: Lynne Rienner Publishers, 2015.

Laine, Carolee. *The War on Poverty.* Minneapolis, MN: Abdo Educational Publishers, 2016.

Landriault, Catherine Andrea, and the Client Action Committee. *I May Not Have a Home...But I Have Rights.* Calgary, AB: CreateSpace Independent Publishing Platform, 2017.

Lowrey, Sassafras, ed. *Kicked Out.* Ypsilanti, MI: Homofactus Press LLC, 2010.

Roberts, Dr. Jillian, and Jaime Casap. *On Our Street: Our First Talk About Poverty.* Victoria, BC: Orca Book Publishers, 2018.

Books—Fiction

Applegate, Katherine. *Crenshaw.* New York, NY: Feiwel & Friends, 2015.

Bunting, Eve. *Fly Away Home.* New York, NY: Clarion Books, 1993.

DiSalvo-Ryan, DyAnne. *Uncle Willie and the Soup Kitchen.* New York, NY: Harper Collins, 1997.

Flake, Sharon. *Money Hungry.* New York, NY: Little, Brown Books for Young Readers, 2019.

Gunning, Monica, and Elaine Pedlar. *A Shelter in Our Car.* San Francisco, CA: Children's Book Press, 2014.

Gunti, Erin. *A Place to Stay: A Shelter Story.* Cambridge, MA: Barefoot Books, 2019.

Hesse, Karen. *Just Juice.* Toronto, ON: Scholastic Signature, 1999.

Kulling, Monica. *Aunt Pearl.* Toronto, ON: Groundwood Books, 2019.

Nielsen, Susin. *No Fixed Address.* Toronto, ON: Tundra Books, 2018.

Peterson, Lois. *Three Good Things.* Victoria, BC: Orca Book Publishers, 2015.

Sturgis, Brenda Reeves. *Still a Family.* Park Ridge, IL: Albert Whitman & Company, 2017.

Upjohn, Rebecca. *Lily and the Paperman.* Toronto, ON: Second Story Press, 2007.

Watson, Cristy. *Living Rough.* Victoria, BC: Orca Book Publishers, 2011.

Williams, Laura. *The Can Man.* New York, NY: Lee & Low Books, 2017.

Online

Canadian Observatory on Homelessness: Homeless Hub (Canada): homelesshub.ca

Feeding America: feedingamerica.org

Feeding Pets of the Homeless: petsofthehomeless.org

Homelessadvice.com

Homelessness Facts for Kids: kids.kiddle.co/Homelessness

Liam's Lunches of Love: liamslove.com

National Alliance to End Homelessness: endhomelessness.org

ACKNOWLEDGMENTS

Everyone I've met who struggles with homelessness and poverty, or who helps people who do, contributed to this book. Their courage, energy and commitment is an example to those who believe that everyone deserves a safe, secure home.

I thank everyone who shared their story, gave me information or let me know where and how I could learn more. Special thanks to Kaitlin Schwan, senior researcher with the Canadian Observatory on Homelessness, for her valuable input, and to editor Kirstie Hudson, who helped me make this book the best it can be. And, as always, my thanks to Douglas Brunt, my first and best reader.

Ignoring homelessness will not make it go away. It takes governments, social service agencies and people working together to find solutions for the thousands of people in North America who live without safe, secure homes.
CHIP SOMODEVILLA/GETTY IMAGES

INDEX

*Page numbers in **bold** indicate an image caption.*

LOIS PETERSON is the award-winning author of eight books of fiction for children and numerous short stories, essays and articles for adults. She was the executive director of a homeless shelter and worked at a public library for more than 40 years. Lois lives in Nanaimo, British Columbia.

ORCA
Think
Stay Curious!

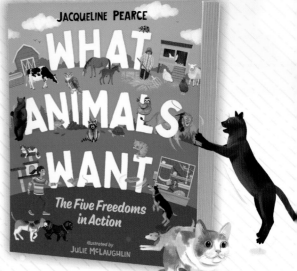

WHAT'S THE BIG IDEA?

The Orca Think series introduces us to the issues making headlines in the world today. It encourages us to question, connect and take action for a better future. With those tools we can all become better citizens. Now that's smart thinking!

UPCOMING TOPICS INCLUDE:

The Right to a Healthy Environment
Wearable Technology
Media Literacy

ORCA